# KIDS ON EARTH

*Wildlife Adventures – Explore The World*
*Octopus - Maldives*

Sensei Paul David

# COPYRIGHT PAGE

Kids On Earth: Wildlife Adventures - Explore The World

Octopus - Maldives

by Sensei Paul David,

Copyright © 2023.

All rights reserved.

978-1-77848-197-0 KoE_WildLife_Amazon_PaperbackBook_maldives_octopus

978-1-77848-196-3 KoE_WildLife_Amazon_eBook_maldives_octopus

978-1-77848-428-5 KoE_Wildlife_Ingram_Paperbackbook_Octopus Paperback

This book is not authorized for free distribution copying.

www.senseipublishing.com

@senseipublishing
#senseipublishing

# Synopsis

This book explored the unique characteristics and behaviors of octopuses in the Maldives. It provided 30 fun facts about these intelligent creatures, from their diet and habitat to their physical features and intelligence. The book also discussed their three hearts, color-changing abilities, and ability to use tools. Through this book, readers gained a greater appreciation for the complex lives of octopuses in the Maldives.

# Get Our FREE Books Now!

kidsonearth.life

kidsonearth.world

# Click Below for Another Book In Each Series

senseipublishing.com/KoE_SERIES

senseipublishing.com/KoE_Wildlife_SERIES

## KoE En Español

senseipublishing.com/KoE_SERIES_SPANISH

www.senseipublishing.com

# Join Our Publishing Journey!

If you would like to receive FUTURE FREE BOOKS and get to know us better, please click www.senseipublishing.com and join our newsletter by entering your email address in the pop-up box.

**Follow Our Blog: senseipauldavid.ca**

Follow/Like/Subscribe: Facebook, Instagram, YouTube: @senseipublishing

Scan the QR Code with your phone or tablet to follow us on social media:

Like / Subscribe / Follow

# Introduction

Welcome to the fascinating world of octopuses! Octopuses are incredibly intelligent creatures that inhabit the depths of the oceans around the world, including the waters of the Maldives. This book will take you on an exciting journey to explore the unique characteristics and behaviors of octopuses in the Maldives. From their diet and habitat to their physical features and intelligence, this book will teach you 30 fun facts about octopuses in the Maldives.

Octopuses in the Maldives have three hearts! The main heart pumps blood to the body while the other two pump it to the gills.

Octopuses in the Maldives can change their color and texture in a matter of seconds to blend in with their surroundings.

Octopuses in the Maldives can squirt water from their siphons to escape from predators.

Octopuses in the Maldives have eight limbs that are lined with suction cups. These suction cups allow them to move quickly and easily over rocks and coral.

Octopuses in the Maldives are carnivores and feed on a variety of small sea creatures such as crabs, shrimp, and fish.

Octopuses in the Maldives have a highly developed brain and are very intelligent creatures.

Octopuses in the Maldives can live up to four years in the wild.

Octopuses in the Maldives mate by using a special arm called a hectocotylus.

Octopuses in the Maldives lay thousands of eggs at once and guard them until they hatch.

Octopuses in the Maldives can lose limbs and regenerate them later.

Octopuses in the Maldives can squirt ink to distract predators.

Octopuses in the Maldives can see color even though they don't have eyes.

Octopuses in the Maldives are nocturnal, meaning they hunt and feed at night.

Octopuses in the Maldives have a beak-like mouth and sharp, parrot-like beak for cracking shells.

Octopuses in the Maldives can navigate their environment by using their sense of smell.

Octopuses in the Maldives can taste with their suckers.

Octopuses in the Maldives have a special type of skin called chromatophores that allow them to change color.

Octopuses in the Maldives can walk on land, but they don't do it often.

Octopuses in the Maldives can squeeze into small spaces due to their lack of a hard outer shell.

Octopuses in the Maldives can use tools to complete tasks, such as opening shells or removing rocks.

Octopuses in the Maldives can communicate with one another using a special type of ink called sepia.

Octopuses in the Maldives can live up to 200 meters deep in the ocean.

Octopuses in the Maldives are solitary creatures and usually prefer to live alone.

Octopuses in the Maldives can be found in a variety of colors, including white, black, brown, and orange.

Octopuses in the Maldives can regrow lost arms, eyes, and other body parts.

Octopuses in the Maldives have a special type of skin called chromatophores that allow them to change color and texture.

Octopuses in the Maldives have a lifespan of up to four years in the wild.

Octopuses in the Maldives are excellent swimmers and can move very quickly in the water.

Octopuses in the Maldives live in shallow coral reefs and can travel up to 100 meters away from their home.

Octopuses in the Maldives are intelligent creatures and can recognize patterns and solve problems.

## Conclusion

Octopuses in the Maldives are fascinating creatures with many unique characteristics and behaviors. From their diet and habitat to their physical features and intelligence, this book has taught you 30 fun facts about octopuses in the Maldives. We hope you have enjoyed learning about these amazing creatures and that you have a greater appreciation for their complex lives.

# Thank you for reading this book!

If you found this book helpful, I would be grateful if you would **post an honest review on Amazon** so this book can reach other supportive readers like you!

All you necd to do is digitally flip to the back and leave your review. Or visit amazon.com/author/senseipauldavid click the correct book cover and click on the blue link next to the yellow stars that say, "customer reviews."

*As always...*

*It's a great day to be alive!*

# Share Our FREE eBooks Now!

kidsonearth.life

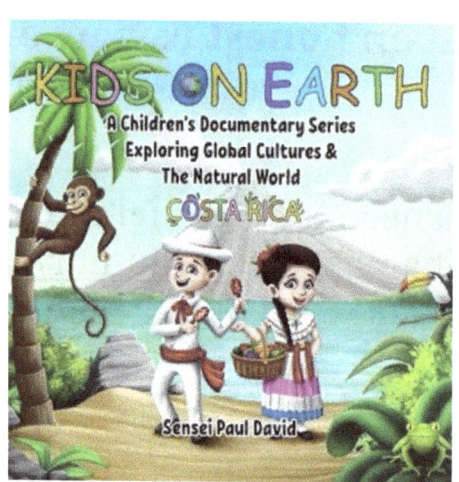

kidsonearth.world

# Click Below for Another Book In Each Series

senseipublishing.com/KoE_SERIES

senseipublishing.com/KoE_Wildlife_SERIES

## KoE En Español

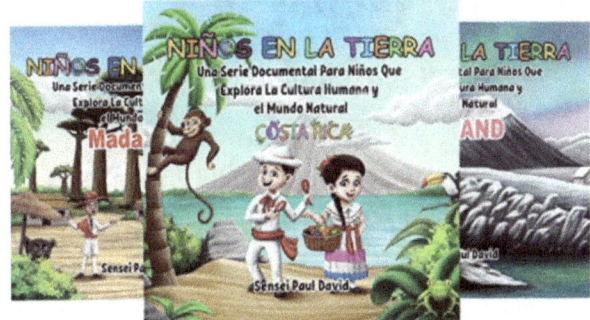

senseipublishing.com/KoE_SERIES_SPANISH

www.senseipublishing.com

www.senseipublishing.com

@senseipublishing
#senseipublishing

Check out our **recommendations** for other books for adults & kids plus other great resources by visiting
www.senseipublishing.com/resources/

# Join Our Publishing Journey!

If you would like to receive FREE BOOKS and special offers, please visit www.senseipublishing.com and join our newsletter by entering your email address in the pop-up box

## Follow Our Engaging Blog NOW!
## senseipauldavid.ca

## Get Our FREE Books Today!

Click & Share the Links Below

## FREE Kids Books

lifeofbailey.senseipublishing.com
kidsonearth.senseipublishing.com

## FREE Self-Development Book

senseiselfdevelopment.senseipublishing.com

**FREE BONUS!!!**
**Experience Over 25 FREE Engaging Guided Meditations!**

Prized Skills & Practices for Adults & Kids. Help Restore Deep Sleep, Lower Stress, Improve Posture, Navigate Uncertainty & More.

Download the Free Insight Timer App and click the link below:
**http://insig.ht/sensei_paul**

# About Sensei Publishing

Sensei Publishing commits itself to helping people of all ages transform into better versions of themselves by providing high-quality and research-based self-development books with an emphasis on mental health and guided meditations. Sensei Publishing offers well-written e-books, audiobooks, paperbacks, and online courses that simplify complicated but practical topics in line with its mission to inspire people toward positive transformation.

It's a great day to be alive!

# About the Author

I create simple & transformative eBooks & Guided Meditations for Adults & Children proven to help navigate uncertainty, solve niche problems & bring families closer together.

I'm a former finance project manager, private pilot, jiu-jitsu instructor, musician & former University of Toronto Fitness Trainer. I prefer a science-based approach to focus on these & other areas in my life to stay humble & hungry to evolve. I hope you enjoy my work and I'd love to hear your feedback.

- It's a great day to be alive!
Sensei Paul David

Scan & Follow/Like/Subscribe: Facebook, Instagram, YouTube: @senseipublishing

Scan using your phone/iPad camera for Social Media
Visit us at www.senseipublishing.com and sign up for our newsletter to learn more about our exciting books and to experience our FREE Guided Meditations for Kids & Adults.

www.ingramcontent.com/pod-product-compliance
Lightning Source LLC
Chambersburg PA
CBHW080616110526
44587CB00040BB/3730